Masks, Mind, And Pain

what i've experienced so far

Amara Everleigh October

BookLeaf
Publishing

India | USA | UK

Made with ❤ on the BookLeaf Publishing Platform
www.bookleafpub.in
www.bookleafpub.com

Dedication

thank you to the ones who tried to be there, even if it didn't work. I appreciate your efforts.

Preface

Hi. This is Amara Everleigh October. I am currently at the age of 12 years old writing this book. I really wanted to share this book with people--including peers, adults, and parents--so they understand what some kids my age have to go through based on other's actions. The way you react to something and why you react to it could really impact any persons life no matter their age.

I've gone through way too much and have been exposed to betrayal I shouldn't have been at my young age and I hope other people can see how empathy and compassion can really make a difference in someones life. And just because someone seems happy on the outside doesn't mean they are on the inside. And just because someone hasn't even started puberty or are at a young age doesn't mean they can't experience what some adults experience too. Thank you so much. Please enjoy this variety of poems I had put together and have put my entire heart and soul into.

Acknowledgements

Thank you to Bookleaf publishing for making this book possible

1. mask

happy day, happy day
(i'm trying my best with my poker face)

the flowers surround, all around
(they start to wilt and follow my frown)

im writing, im writing
(but the poems are about dying)

the mask **cracks**,
unable to keep it in.

2. odd

im the blouse in a closet of dresses
the wine on a table of water

this isn't my right place

the dagger on a counter of knives
a pen in a bag of markers

the thought of being judged everyday

the ruby in a cave of diamonds
a lone star in the night sky

is **torture**.

3. blocked

the world wears a mask
and I only have one task
to try and see behind it

but my mind tries to make it hidden
to write it in a different way than it is written
but still, the vision is way too blurry

i've lost sense in true reality
lost ability for my personal vitality
and I can't even tell what's real or fake

she lied to me for continuous years straight
and she still has me locked behind a gate
and I barely feel true emotions anymore

even if this message may not be as cryptic
my toxic socializations are over acidic
my only two friends are too nuclear

and I can't open up whatever I do
because even to myself, I'm not even true
even therapists don't understand

since it's long, I should conclude
living with the fact that I'll continue to be used

4. illusion

my thoughts were all a lie

some sort of illusion
i believe was a delusion

i want to believe it all again

i finally feel fixed
but my feelings although, are still mixed

but I feel no confusion.

am I ill?
death still hasn't had its fill

yes, it was an illusion.
but i still haven't found truth to my own lies.

5. stacked

As I try to let them go,
there's a feeling inside I just don't know.

When I confronted one,
my hands started shaking,
and my heart kept breaking.

I try to be good, but why's it so hard?
Even when I play, I hold the bad card.

I own a bad hand—
just look at my luck.
I just lost a pair… oh, fuck.

I had a royal flush but didn't play it,
a mistake I regret—how I hate it.

I know it's not healthy,
I know it's bad,
but my grip on loneliness is just sad.

I started the year with a terrible choice,
parting ways with my only two friends—
my voice.

I know it was my decision,
I didn't have to let go,
but I couldn't let this pain grow.

Only now I see how toxic she was,
only now I realize how deep it cut.

I miss them dearly; the pain remains,
but now I know not to trust in vain.

It wasn't her fault—I know she's hurting,
but that didn't give her the right to ruin me.

I'm hurt by my consequences,
I went all in,
it's all I'm known for by my closest kin.

Only known for the toxic ties,
I didn't see the damage behind those lies.

Now I question if my "trauma" is real,
even if I tell someone,
I fear this pain won't heal.

I shared my deepest secrets,
I let them see my pain,

only to watch them weaponize my shame.

Now I live defined by what I've been through,
branded by the past, stuck like glue.

Then it became a joke—
or so I thought,
hard to pretend to be someone I'm not.

The world's number one sociopath,
"Friends" are something I used to have.

Now I'm out of chips,
a terrible play,
they ridicule me in the cruelest ways.

I'm scared to go back,
I start to tremble,
I miss the courage from when I was a rebel.

I wish I could be myself,
not just a card on a shelf,
paralyzed by fear, unable to ask for help.

I'm here all alone,
no place to call home.

So just leave me be,
there's no saving me.

6. thoughts

my thoughts are jabbing against my chest
its my mentality's unwelcome guest

im trying to find a metaphor
but its impossible to find
have you ever thought of the day that you die?

i wanted it soon
like a snack I craved

i really really wanted to
but don't want to cave

7. joke

i'm told critical things,
hurtful truths,
hurtful lies.

whenever i try to make a point,
you deflect with something off,
and i ask myself, "why?

why did i even try when
all you ever do is not listen,
and make false claims?

you call them jokes—repeatedly,
but they've hurt my community,
they've hurt my home.

and to your homophobic "jokes,"
i'm left prone.

8. deprived

i lay in my bed,
dead, bone tired

my mind,
eating me alive.

my soul,
deprived

the music isn't workin'
that I know for certain

the spirits are all lurking
all over my mind

there it goes...
bye-bye, time.

9. cage

behind the bars of my enclosed mind,
i've lost the keys
in an endless breeze.

my thoughts turn to worries—
am I good enough?
not surely.

i try to piece it all together,
but it feels like a never-ending nether,
a puzzle that refuses to be whole,
a labyrinth within my soul.

and no matter how hard I try,
i can never seem to find
my true sanity.

10. awake

my eyes are closed,
yet conscious.

i'm awake,
but dreaming.

my mind is open,
locked in.

is this necessary?
detachment is scary.

my body goes numb,
yet I'm still feeling.

i'm awake.
i think.

11. defined

who and what i am is not a choice,
not a want,
nor a "sickness" i caught.

it's not a phase,
not something i hyperfixate on
to receive constant hate for.

it's not something to mock,
not something to hurt someone for—
for who they are, down to their core.

it's not a religion,
nor a belief.

my identity is not a joke,
it's who i define as my whole life—
defining who i love and why.

it's someone i am,
not someone i had.

12. lunch

as I listen to their burdens and worries
feelings of relate start to scurry

i say I'm an empath, and i very am surely
but then, it's everything there i start to bury

attacks that physically hurt
i guess it helps teach me to learn and learn

but leaving the bottle shut
and thoughts that would not budge

is what my anxiety eats for lunch.

13. problems

suck it in
don't let the pain show
while all of my insecurities continue grow

they point it out like it's a joke
but just a word, then I'm broke

put on a smile
say it's okay
like nothing is terrible everyday

four hours straight doesn't even work
the therapy not therapeutic as it occurs

they say it's puberty
it probably is
but I don't want to blow my problems away with a kiss.

they all seem fake
and one word all it takes

why won't my problems grow?
i need more ways to cope

i'm growing out of it
but it keeps me company
in my life, will I be my one and only?

but my problems don't seem real
it's js a gift with an open seal

maybe I'm the one whose fake
and I guess I'll continue wearing all these masks I made

14. angel dust

do you know the feeling?

laughing while sobbing,
the voices start fighting,
and they never stop dying.

it's worse than you think.

you're falling apart,
hit by the dart,
tainted by angel dust.

15. loneliness

the room is empty,
and my skin is shedding.

nobody else is here—
just me, to judge myself.

trying to build the bricks,
all alone, eating sticks.

will anyone notice...?

16. home?

as I arrive in this new place,
knowing I'll be here for days... and days.

at first, I feel nothing—
neutral, and that's something.

but then,

anywhere I look,
anywhere I go,

there's something that reminds me of home.

and I'm hit by a bullet every time someone says:
"You are home."

I'm not.

17. grief

as I listen to the news I've just received,
this is something I never believed.

gone forever?
now it's finally never.

curling up in my bed,
mental scars left all over my body.

pillows wet for days,
every night, I drown in the lake—
the one I've created myself.

18. shatter

as I write on the thin, fragile loose-leaf,
I turn into glass.

the pressure turns on me—
a diamond, scared I may not surpass.

and the diamond shatters,
finally, at last.

the adrenaline rising,
until I finally fail.

19. back

I am going to come back,
finally, at last.
but seeing their faces won't make me laugh.

i'm scared of them all—
i don't know why.
i hope they'll see, in the glimpse of my eye,
that I've changed.

i was a jerk,
yes, I know.
but I want them to see how much I've grown.

they're just gonna use me,
just for my money.
but everyone else says, "honey, don't worry."

"it'll be fine."
"get out of the house."
but how will I,
if I feel like a mouse?

people suck.
i guess it's been established,

because all they do is fill me with sadness.

no matter how loving,
no matter how kind,
i'm always gonna think there's something negative in
your mind.

when I say it, I sound pessimistic, maybe petty—
but they don't know the things I see aren't so pretty.

i just really hope they've changed when I come back—
which is a very, **very** minimal chance.

20. fake

I know what it's like to have a friend I love,
one I'd go to, BFF, till the heavens above.

until I realized she was only faking—
it makes me want to shatter, to start breaking.

it's already been a year,
but just thinking about her still makes me shed a tear.

she made my heart warm,
calmed my internal storm.

but she was the one I truly loved, as a genuine friend.

it may sound romantic, but it really isn't—
she was the person who made me less livid.

I'm even tearing up, writing this poem—
I wish she knew how much I'd do for her,
before she ruined me.

21. I've tried

I've treated all with respect,
I've treated none with less,
and this is what I receive?

I interrupt none,
I stopped moving my tongue,
and yet, I'm insulted for the nicest form of me.

I've changed, I promise,
I've been nothing but honest,
but it's so obviously clear you can't see any of it.

I agree with you, no matter how I'm treated.
I've gotten bruises and scars for your own
achievements,
and I still don't understand why you don't understand.

I really, really tried.
I've cut, I've loved, I've cried,
and I finally broke.

I've tried to be nice,
and tried to be wise.

I've tried to be kind,
and tried to be a light.

I've tried talking to you,
and tried seeing you through.

I've tried creating a spark,
and tried being light when it's dark.

I've tried hurting myself,
and tried giving you my wealth.

I've tried hurting you too,
and tried something new.

I've tried letting you go,
and tried saying no.

I've tried putting up boundaries,
and tried coping profoundly.

I've tried escaping the cage,
and tried fighting my rage.

And you say I didn't have to do it,
but yes, I did.
I needed to be seen, because you were the only ones in

my life I could talk to—
but you never really cared.

I know we can't be people pleasers,
but you were all I had there.
Because anyone I talked to wouldn't listen.

I've tried so hard.
So hard.

Two years. Maybe three.

I put up with your shit for years,
letting it happen over and over again,
accepting your words saying, "It's a joke."
I've even tried letting go.
But I just can't.

Why can't I?
Even I don't know.

www.ingramcontent.com/pod-product-compliance
Lightning Source LLC
LaVergne TN
LVHW051245200726

843510LV00011B/1688